The
United States Presidents

ANDREW JOHNSON

ABDO Publishing Company

Megan M. Gunderson

visit us at
www.abdopublishing.com

Published by ABDO Publishing Company, 8000 West 78th Street, Edina, Minnesota 55439.
Copyright © 2009 by Abdo Consulting Group, Inc. International copyrights reserved in all
countries. No part of this book may be reproduced in any form without written permission from the
publisher. The Checkerboard Library™ is a trademark and logo of ABDO Publishing Company.

Printed in the United States.

Cover Photo: Getty Images
Interior Photos: Alamy pp. 11, 29; AP Images p. 9; Getty Images pp. 5, 13, 19, 21, 25;
    iStockphoto p. 32; Library of Congress pp. 15, 16, 22, 27; National Archives pp. 17, 26;
    National Park Service p. 12; Picture History p. 28

Editor: BreAnn Rumsch
Art Direction & Cover Design: Neil Klinepier
Interior Design: Neil Klinepier

Library of Congress Cataloging-in-Publication Data

Gunderson, Megan M., 1981-
  Andrew Johnson / Megan M. Gunderson.
    p. cm. -- (The United States presidents)
  Includes index.
  ISBN 978-1-60453-461-0
  1. Johnson, Andrew, 1808-1875--Juvenile literature. 2. Presidents--United States--Biography--
Juvenile literature. I. Title.

  E667.G86 2009
  973.8'1092--dc22
  [B]

                              2008030960

CONTENTS

ANDREW JOHNSON

Andrew Johnson was the seventeenth president of the United States. Before taking office, he was Abraham Lincoln's vice president. After the American **Civil War** ended in 1865, President Lincoln was **assassinated**. Johnson then became president.

Johnson tried to follow the rules of the U.S. **Constitution**. He favored states' rights over increasing the power of the federal government. Because of this, President Johnson and Congress often disagreed. They argued about how to run the country after the war.

While president, Johnson challenged a law Congress had passed. Congress felt he had broken the law. So in 1868, Johnson became the first president to be **impeached**. The Senate voted to decide if he should be removed from office. By just one vote, the Senate decided to keep Johnson in office.

Johnson was not nominated for a second term. After leaving office, he became the only former president elected to the U.S. Senate. Johnson had a difficult presidency. Yet he was a lifelong politician who always fought hard for his beliefs.

TIMELINE

1808 - On December 29, Andrew Johnson was born in Raleigh, North Carolina.

1827 - On May 17, Johnson married Eliza McCardle; Johnson opened his own tailor shop.

1829 - In Tennessee, Johnson was elected to the Greeneville town council.

1835 - Johnson began serving in the Tennessee House of Representatives.

1841 - Johnson was elected to the Tennessee state senate.

1843 - Johnson began serving in the U.S. House of Representatives.

1853 - Johnson became governor of Tennessee.

1857 - Johnson began serving in the U.S. Senate.

1861 - The American Civil War began on April 12; on June 8, Tennessee voted to secede.

1862 - President Abraham Lincoln appointed Johnson military governor of Tennessee; the Homestead Act passed.

1864 - Johnson was elected vice president under Lincoln.

1865 - The Civil War ended on April 9; on April 15, President Lincoln died; that day, Johnson became the seventeenth U.S. president; Johnson announced his Reconstruction plans.

1867 - Congress passed the Tenure of Office Act; Nebraska became the thirty-seventh U.S. state.

1868 - The U.S. House of Representatives impeached President Johnson, but the Senate voted to keep him in office.

1875 - Johnson was elected to the U.S. Senate; on July 31, Andrew Johnson died.

DID YOU KNOW?

Legend has it that Eliza McCardle fell in love with Andrew Johnson at first sight. When she saw him arrive in Greeneville, Tennessee, she told her friends, "There goes my beau, girls." She had not even met him yet! But soon after, they fell in love and married.

While Johnson was president, the United States purchased what would become Alaska. They paid Russia just over seven million dollars for the land. That is just two cents per acre!

When former president Johnson returned to the Senate, he was welcomed with a bouquet of flowers on his desk.

In 1868, Johnson became the first U.S. president to be impeached. No other president was impeached until Bill Clinton in 1998.

YOUNG ANDREW

Andrew Johnson was born on December 29, 1808, in Raleigh, North Carolina. Andrew had an older brother named William. His older sister, Elizabeth, died in childhood.

Their father, Jacob, had various jobs. He worked at an inn and a bank. He was also the town bell ringer. Their mother, Mary "Polly" McDonough, was a weaver. Still, the family was poor.

When Andrew was just three, his father died. Jacob had jumped into a pond to save three men from drowning. The incident weakened him, and he died in January 1812. Later, Andrew's mother remarried.

Growing up, Andrew enjoyed playing ball, swimming, and fishing. He also was very interested in learning. However, his family could not afford to send him to school. So, he and his brother soon became **apprentices**.

FAST FACTS

BORN - December 29, 1808
WIFE - Eliza McCardle
(1810–1876)
CHILDREN - 5
POLITICAL PARTY - Democrat
AGE AT INAUGURATION - 56
YEARS SERVED - 1865–1869
VICE PRESIDENT - None
DIED - July 31, 1875, age 66

Andrew's birthplace

TAILOR'S APPRENTICE

When Andrew was 14, he became a tailor's **apprentice**. Andrew's contract said he would work for James J. Selby until he was 21. William was also Selby's apprentice.

At Selby's, Andrew became known for his interest in learning. He learned to read. And, he enjoyed listening to visitors discuss politics.

A local man often read out loud as Andrew worked. The man read from a book of speeches by American and English **statesmen**. He later gave the book to Andrew. Andrew kept it for the rest of his life.

When Andrew was 15, he ran away from his job. Selby offered a ten dollar reward for his return. Andrew traveled from town to town. He worked for tailors in Carthage, North Carolina, and Laurens, South Carolina. But no one was supposed to hire a runaway apprentice. Andrew was always in danger of being caught.

Eventually, Andrew returned home to Raleigh. Without a large payment, Selby refused to release him from his contract. Andrew could not afford to buy his freedom. So, he decided to leave North Carolina. In 1826, Andrew moved to Greeneville, Tennessee.

After Andrew became president, he claimed he could still sew a coat!

FAMILY AND WORK

In Greeneville, Johnson met Eliza McCardle. They married on May 17, 1827. The Johnsons had five children. They were named Martha, Charles, Mary, Robert, and Andrew.

Also in 1827, Johnson opened his own tailor shop. He was a good tailor. Many people came to see him. They often discussed politics. Mrs. Johnson read to her husband while he worked. She helped him improve his reading and writing skills. Johnson also studied the U.S. **Constitution**.

Eliza Johnson attended school at the Rhea Academy in Greeneville.

Johnson became a good speaker. He loved **debating**. In fact, he joined debating societies at two nearby colleges. Johnson stood out as a leader in the town. He soon decided to become involved in politics.

Johnson led many political discussions at his tailor shop.

TENNESSEE POLITICIAN

In 1829, Johnson was elected to the Greeneville Town Council. On the council, he represented working-class people. Soon, Johnson was elected mayor of Greeneville.

Next, Johnson was elected to the Tennessee House of Representatives. As a **Democrat**, he served from 1835 to 1837. He served again from 1839 to 1841.

Johnson became known for his energetic speeches and his support of laborers. He voted against expanding railroads. He felt they harmed inns and other businesses. Johnson also fought wasteful government spending. In 1841, Johnson was elected to the Tennessee state senate.

Next, Johnson was elected to the U.S. House of Representatives. He served for ten years beginning in 1843.

There, Johnson introduced a homestead bill. The bill would have given land in the West to settlers for free. However, Southern politicians defeated the bill. They feared it would reduce government earnings from land sales.

Johnson's excellent public speaking skills helped him succeed in politics.

Johnson also favored states' rights. So, he supported the Compromise of 1850. Part of the compromise allowed certain new states to decide if they would allow slavery.

In 1853, Johnson became governor of Tennessee. He was reelected in 1855. As governor, Johnson helped improve the public school system. He also became a member of the state's new Agricultural Bureau. In this way, he continued helping farmers.

LOYAL SENATOR

Johnson continued his political career. In 1857, he became a U.S. senator. By now, slavery had become a major issue in the United States. Northerners wanted to end it. But Southerners wanted to keep it. As a senator, Johnson continued to support a state's right to allow slavery.

Abraham Lincoln

In November 1860, Abraham Lincoln was elected president. The Southern states feared President Lincoln would not support their right to own slaves. So a few weeks later, Southern states began **seceding**. They formed a new country called the Confederate States of America.

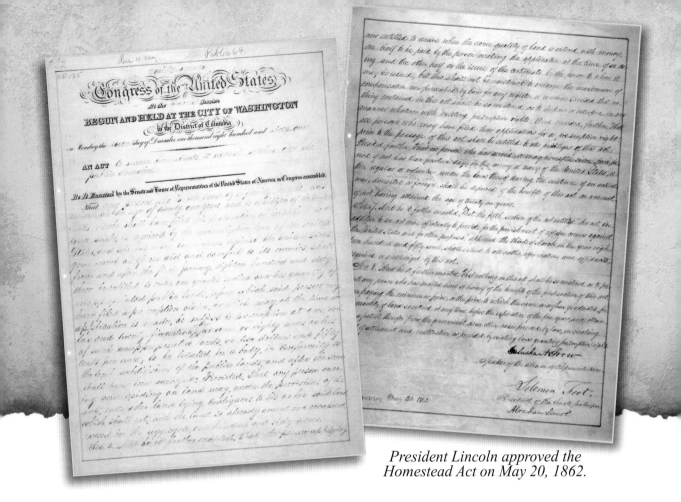

President Lincoln approved the Homestead Act on May 20, 1862.

Johnson was a Southerner and a slave owner. However, he was against **secession**. He soon became the only Southern senator to remain in the U.S. Senate. There, he kept fighting for his homestead bill. Southern politicians were no longer there to oppose it. So in 1862, the Homestead Act finally became law.

Meanwhile, the American **Civil War** began on April 12, 1861. On June 8, Tennessee voted to join the Confederacy. Johnson's family was then forced from his Tennessee home. The Confederates seized Johnson's property.

The states that remained in the United States were now called the Union. Eventually, the Union began regaining control of Tennessee. In March 1862, President Lincoln made Johnson the military governor of Tennessee. Johnson's job was to help Tennessee rejoin the Union. He moved to Nashville, where his family joined him.

As governor, Johnson took control of Tennessee's railroads. He had people arrested for not supporting the federal government. Johnson also closed anti-Union newspapers.

In 1864, Johnson was chosen to run as Lincoln's vice president. Lincoln was a **Republican**. He wanted a loyal **Democrat** as his **running mate**. This helped show people that the national government represented everyone.

The Democrats nominated General George B. McClellan. His running mate was Representative George H. Pendleton. Running as the Union Party, Lincoln and Johnson easily defeated their opponents. They received 212 electoral votes. McClellan and Pendleton received just 21!

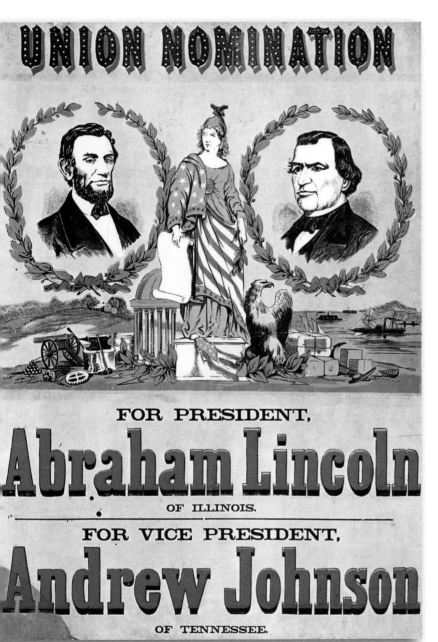

FOR PRESIDENT,

Abraham Lincoln

OF ILLINOIS.

FOR VICE PRESIDENT,

Andrew Johnson

OF TENNESSEE.

On April 9, 1865, the South surrendered. The North had won the **Civil War**. Yet before the country could begin healing, tragedy struck.

On April 14, 1865, actor John Wilkes Booth shot President Lincoln. He wanted to avenge the South. Abraham Lincoln died the next day. A few hours later, Johnson was sworn in as president.

Lincoln and Johnson received more than 400,000 more popular votes than McClellan and Pendleton.

RECONSTRUCTION

President Johnson and Congress now faced a difficult task. They had to bring the Southern states back into the Union. This is called Reconstruction.

Johnson soon announced his plans for an easy, smooth reunion. Each Southern state could return if it wrote a new state **constitution** that banned slavery. And each state had to approve the Thirteenth **Amendment**. This also banned slavery. Each state also had to formally withdraw its act of **secession**. In addition, Southerners had to swear an oath of loyalty to the United States.

By December 1865, nearly every Southern state had completed Johnson's requirements. However, many Southern leaders now passed laws called black codes.

Each state's codes were slightly different. Yet all black codes limited the rights of **freedmen**. They could not have skilled jobs or attend state schools. They could not own property or weapons, either.

PRESIDENT JOHNSON'S CABINET

APRIL 15, 1865–
MARCH 4, 1869

- **STATE** – William H. Seward
- **TREASURY** – Hugh McCulloch
- **WAR** – Edwin M. Stanton
  John M. Schofield (from June 1, 1868)
- **NAVY** – Gideon Welles
- **ATTORNEY GENERAL** – James Speed
  Henry Stanbery (from July 23, 1866)
  William M. Evarts (from July 20, 1868)
- **INTERIOR** – John P. Usher
  James Harlan (from May 15, 1865)
  Orville H. Browning (from September 1, 1866)

Congress passed its series of
Reconstruction Acts even though
Johnson had vetoed them.

Many Northern congressmen were against Johnson's Reconstruction plans and the black codes. So in 1866 and 1868, Congress voted to extend the **Freedmen**'s Bureau.

Congress had formed this organization before the **Civil War** had ended. Originally, it was meant to give land to freedmen. Now, it would also provide them with food, medicine, and education.

In 1866, Congress also passed the **Civil Rights** Act. This law defined U.S. citizens as anyone born in the United States. It gave freedmen the right to own land and testify in court.

President Johnson **vetoed** the Freedmen's Bureau and the Civil Rights Act. He felt they violated states' rights. For the first time in history, Congress voted against presidential vetoes. Both acts became law.

Congress then protected the Civil Rights Act with a new **amendment**. The Fourteenth Amendment made all former slaves U.S. citizens. Johnson fought the amendment, but lost.

In 1867, Congress passed a series of Reconstruction Acts. New Southern state governments had to be formed. Southern states had to approve state **constitutions**. These had to guarantee voting rights for all men. The states also had to approve the Fourteenth Amendment. Afterward, Congress would let them rejoin the Union.

IMPEACHMENT

Republican congressmen feared President Johnson would interfere with their Reconstruction plans. So on March 2, 1867, Congress passed the Tenure of Office Act.

Now, anyone the Senate approved for office could not be removed from office without Senate approval. The act would stop Johnson from firing Republican supporters. This included **Secretary of War** Edwin M. Stanton.

Johnson **vetoed** this bill. He felt it gave Congress too much power over the president. But Congress voted against the veto. The Tenure of Office Act became law.

President Johnson felt a duty to challenge the law. So on August 12, 1867, he removed Stanton from office. In December, the Senate refused to approve the removal.

Then on February 21, 1868, Johnson again removed Stanton from office. So, the House of Representatives accused Johnson of disobeying the Tenure of Office Act.

On February 24, the House voted 126 to 47 to **impeach** President Johnson. This was a first in U.S. presidential history. Next, the Senate held a trial to decide whether to remove Johnson from office.

Edwin M. Stanton served in the cabinets of three presidents. They were James Buchanan, Abraham Lincoln, and Andrew Johnson.

On May 16, 1868, each senator voted Johnson guilty or not guilty.

President Johnson's trial began in the U.S. Senate on March 30, 1868. His lawyers claimed he had the right to test whether the Tenure of Office Act was **constitutional**.

On May 16, the Senate voted on Johnson's fate. Two-thirds of the senators had to vote against Johnson to remove him from office. Thirty-five senators voted against Johnson. Nineteen voted for him. President Johnson won by just one vote.

Reconstruction and **impeachment** kept President Johnson busy. However, he also oversaw the growth of the nation. On March 1, 1867, Nebraska became the thirty-seventh U.S. state.

Around the same time, **Secretary of State** William H. Seward arranged a large land purchase. The United States gained what would become Alaska from Russia.

Still, the **Democratic** Party did not nominate Johnson for a second term. Instead, party members chose former New York governor Horatio Seymour. Seymour

William H. Seward served as secretary of state for eight years under Lincoln and Johnson.

lost the 1868 election to **Republican** Ulysses S. Grant. Then in March 1869, Johnson left the White House.

AFTER THE WHITE HOUSE

Johnson returned home to Greeneville, Tennessee. There, he was happy to be surrounded by his family. Still, he missed the excitement of being in politics.

So in 1869, Johnson ran for the U.S. Senate. He lost the election. Yet he did not give up on politics. In 1872, Johnson ran for a seat in the U.S. House of Representatives. He lost that election, too.

Then in 1875, Johnson was elected to the U.S. Senate. He is the only former president to become a senator. Johnson began his term on March 4.

Johnson was buried with an American flag wrapped around him.

A few months later, Johnson became very ill. While visiting his daughter Mary, he suffered two **strokes**. On July 31, 1875, Andrew Johnson died.

Andrew Johnson had a difficult presidency. He faced many challenges during Reconstruction. Yet he maintained his lifelong devotion to the U.S. **Constitution**. He was buried with a copy of it as his pillow.

Today, Johnson's Greeneville home is part of the Andrew Johnson National Historic Site.

OFFICE OF THE PRESIDENT

BRANCHES OF GOVERNMENT

The U.S. government is divided into three branches. They are the executive, legislative, and judicial branches. This division is called a separation of powers. Each branch has some power over the others. This is called a system of checks and balances.

EXECUTIVE BRANCH

The executive branch enforces laws. It is made up of the president, the vice president, and the president's cabinet. The president represents the United States around the world. He or she oversees relations with other countries and signs treaties. The president signs bills into law and appoints officials and federal judges. He or she also leads the military and manages government workers.

LEGISLATIVE BRANCH

The legislative branch makes laws, maintains the military, and regulates trade. It also has the power to declare war. This branch consists of the Senate and the House of Representatives. Together, these two houses make up Congress. Each state has two senators. A state's population determines the number of representatives it has.

JUDICIAL BRANCH

The judicial branch interprets laws. It consists of district courts, courts of appeals, and the Supreme Court. District courts try cases. If a person disagrees with a trial's outcome, he or she may appeal. If the courts of appeals support the ruling, a person may appeal to the Supreme Court. The Supreme Court also makes sure that laws follow the U.S. Constitution.

QUALIFICATIONS FOR OFFICE

To be president, a person must meet three requirements. A candidate must be at least 35 years old and a natural-born U.S. citizen. He or she must also have lived in the United States for at least 14 years.

ELECTORAL COLLEGE

The U.S. presidential election is an indirect election. Voters from each state choose electors to represent them in the Electoral College. The number of electors from each state is based on population. Each elector has one electoral vote. Electors are pledged to cast their vote for the candidate who receives the highest number of popular votes in their state. A candidate must receive the majority of Electoral College votes to win.

TERM OF OFFICE

Each president may be elected to two four-year terms. Sometimes, a president may only be elected once. This happens if he or she served more than two years of the previous president's term.

The presidential election is held on the Tuesday after the first Monday in November. The president is sworn in on January 20 of the following year. At that time, he or she takes the oath of office:

I do solemnly swear (or affirm) that I will faithfully execute the office of President of the United States, and will to the best of my ability, preserve, protect and defend the Constitution of the United States.

LINE OF SUCCESSION

The Presidential Succession Act of 1947 defines who becomes president if the president cannot serve. The vice president is first in the line of succession. Next are the Speaker of the House and the President Pro Tempore of the Senate. If none of these individuals is able to serve, the office falls to the president's cabinet members. They would take office in the order in which each department was created:

Secretary of State
Secretary of the Treasury
Secretary of Defense
Attorney General
Secretary of the Interior
Secretary of Agriculture
Secretary of Commerce
Secretary of Labor
Secretary of Health and Human Services
Secretary of Housing and Urban Development
Secretary of Transportation
Secretary of Energy
Secretary of Education
Secretary of Veterans Affairs
Secretary of Homeland Security

BENEFITS

- While in office, the president receives a salary of $400,000 each year. He or she lives in the White House and has 24-hour Secret Service protection.

- The president may travel on a Boeing 747 jet called Air Force One. The airplane can accommodate 70 passengers. It has kitchens, a dining room, sleeping areas, and a conference room. It also has fully equipped offices with the latest communications systems. Air Force One can fly halfway around the world before needing to refuel. It can even refuel in flight!

- If the president wishes to travel by car, he or she uses Cadillac One. Cadillac One is a Cadillac Deville. It has been modified with heavy armor and communications systems. The president takes Cadillac One along when visiting other countries if secure transportation will be needed.

- The president also travels on a helicopter called Marine One. Like the presidential car, Marine One accompanies the president when traveling abroad if necessary.

- Sometimes, the president needs to get away and relax with family and friends. Camp David is the official presidential retreat. It is located in the cool, wooded mountains in Maryland. The U.S. Navy maintains the retreat, and the U.S. Marine Corps keeps it secure. The camp offers swimming, tennis, golf, and hiking.

- When the president leaves office, he or she receives Secret Service protection for ten more years. He or she also receives a yearly pension of $191,300 and funding for office space, supplies, and staff.

PRESIDENTS AND THEIR TERMS

PRESIDENT	PARTY	TOOK OFFICE	LEFT OFFICE	TERMS SERVED	VICE PRESIDENT
George Washington	None	April 30, 1789	March 4, 1797	Two	John Adams
John Adams	Federalist	March 4, 1797	March 4, 1801	One	Thomas Jefferson
Thomas Jefferson	Democratic-Republican	March 4, 1801	March 4, 1809	Two	Aaron Burr, George Clinton
James Madison	Democratic-Republican	March 4, 1809	March 4, 1817	Two	George Clinton, Elbridge Gerry
James Monroe	Democratic-Republican	March 4, 1817	March 4, 1825	Two	Daniel D. Tompkins
John Quincy Adams	Democratic-Republican	March 4, 1825	March 4, 1829	One	John C. Calhoun
Andrew Jackson	Democrat	March 4, 1829	March 4, 1837	Two	John C. Calhoun, Martin Van Buren
Martin Van Buren	Democrat	March 4, 1837	March 4, 1841	One	Richard M. Johnson
William H. Harrison	Whig	March 4, 1841	April 4, 1841	Died During First Term	John Tyler
John Tyler	Whig	April 6, 1841	March 4, 1845	Completed Harrison's Term	Office Vacant
James K. Polk	Democrat	March 4, 1845	March 4, 1849	One	George M. Dallas
Zachary Taylor	Whig	March 5, 1849	July 9, 1850	Died During First Term	Millard Fillmore

PRESIDENTS 1–12, 1789–1850

PRESIDENT	PARTY	TOOK OFFICE	LEFT OFFICE	TERMS SERVED	VICE PRESIDENT
Millard Fillmore	Whig	July 10, 1850	March 4, 1853	Completed Taylor's Term	Office Vacant
Franklin Pierce	Democrat	March 4, 1853	March 4, 1857	One	William R.D. King
James Buchanan	Democrat	March 4, 1857	March 4, 1861	One	John C. Breckinridge
Abraham Lincoln	Republican	March 4, 1861	April 15, 1865	Served One Term, Died During Second Term	Hannibal Hamlin, Andrew Johnson
Andrew Johnson	Democrat	April 15, 1865	March 4, 1869	Completed Lincoln's Second Term	Office Vacant
Ulysses S. Grant	Republican	March 4, 1869	March 4, 1877	Two	Schuyler Colfax, Henry Wilson
Rutherford B. Hayes	Republican	March 3, 1877	March 4, 1881	One	William A. Wheeler
James A. Garfield	Republican	March 4, 1881	September 19, 1881	Died During First Term	Chester Arthur
Chester Arthur	Republican	September 20, 1881	March 4, 1885	Completed Garfield's Term	Office Vacant
Grover Cleveland	Democrat	March 4, 1885	March 4, 1889	One	Thomas A. Hendricks
Benjamin Harrison	Republican	March 4, 1889	March 4, 1893	One	Levi P. Morton
Grover Cleveland	Democrat	March 4, 1893	March 4, 1897	One	Adlai E. Stevenson
William McKinley	Republican	March 4, 1897	September 14, 1901	Served One Term, Died During Second Term	Garret A. Hobart, Theodore Roosevelt

PRESIDENT	PARTY	TOOK OFFICE	LEFT OFFICE	TERMS SERVED	VICE PRESIDENT
Theodore Roosevelt	Republican	September 14, 1901	March 4, 1909	Completed McKinley's Second Term, Served One Term	Office Vacant, Charles Fairbanks
William Taft	Republican	March 4, 1909	March 4, 1913	One	James S. Sherman
Woodrow Wilson	Democrat	March 4, 1913	March 4, 1921	Two	Thomas R. Marshall
Warren G. Harding	Republican	March 4, 1921	August 2, 1923	Died During First Term	Calvin Coolidge
Calvin Coolidge	Republican	August 3, 1923	March 4, 1929	Completed Harding's Term, Served One Term	Office Vacant, Charles Dawes
Herbert Hoover	Republican	March 4, 1929	March 4, 1933	One	Charles Curtis
Franklin D. Roosevelt	Democrat	March 4, 1933	April 12, 1945	Served Three Terms, Died During Fourth Term	John Nance Garner, Henry A. Wallace, Harry S. Truman
Harry S. Truman	Democrat	April 12, 1945	January 20, 1953	Completed Roosevelt's Fourth Term, Served One Term	Office Vacant, Alben Barkley
Dwight D. Eisenhower	Republican	January 20, 1953	January 20, 1961	Two	Richard Nixon
John F. Kennedy	Democrat	January 20, 1961	November 22, 1963	Died During First Term	Lyndon B. Johnson
Lyndon B. Johnson	Democrat	November 22, 1963	January 20, 1969	Completed Kennedy's Term, Served One Term	Office Vacant, Hubert H. Humphrey
Richard Nixon	Republican	January 20, 1969	August 9, 1974	Completed First Term, Resigned During Second Term	Spiro T. Agnew, Gerald Ford

PRESIDENTS 26–37, 1901–1974

PRESIDENT	PARTY	TOOK OFFICE	LEFT OFFICE	TERMS SERVED	VICE PRESIDENT
Gerald Ford	Republican	August 9, 1974	January 20, 1977	Completed Nixon's Second Term	Nelson A. Rockefeller
Jimmy Carter	Democrat	January 20, 1977	January 20, 1981	One	Walter Mondale
Ronald Reagan	Republican	January 20, 1981	January 20, 1989	Two	George H.W. Bush
George H.W. Bush	Republican	January 20, 1989	January 20, 1993	One	Dan Quayle
Bill Clinton	Democrat	January 20, 1993	January 20, 2001	Two	Al Gore
George W. Bush	Republican	January 20, 2001	January 20, 2009	Two	Dick Cheney
Barack Obama	Democrat	January 20, 2009			Joe Biden

"The life of a republic lies certainly in the energy, virtue, and intelligence of its citizens." Andrew Johnson

WRITE TO THE PRESIDENT

You may write to the president at:

**The White House
1600 Pennsylvania Avenue NW
Washington, DC 20500**

You may e-mail the president at:

comments@whitehouse.gov

GLOSSARY

amendment - a change to a country's constitution.

apprentice - a person who learns a trade or a craft from a skilled worker.

assassinate - to murder a very important person, usually for political reasons.

civil rights - the individual rights of a citizen, such as the right to vote or freedom of speech.

civil war - a war between groups in the same country. The United States of America and the Confederate States of America fought a civil war from 1861 to 1865.

constitution - the laws that govern a country or a state. The U.S. Constitution is the laws that govern the United States. Something relating to or following the laws of a constitution is constitutional.

debate - a contest in which two sides argue for or against something.

Democrat - a member of the Democratic political party. When Andrew Johnson was president, Democrats supported farmers and landowners.

freedman - a person freed from slavery.

impeach - to charge a public official with misconduct in office.

Republican - a member of the Republican political party. When Andrew Johnson was president, Republicans supported business and strong government.

running mate - a candidate running for a lower-rank position on an election ticket, especially the candidate for vice president.

secede - to break away from a group. Secession is the act of formally breaking away.

secretary of state - a member of the president's cabinet who handles relations with other countries.

secretary of war - a member of the president's cabinet who handles the nation's defense.

statesman - one who has knowledge of government and is often involved in shaping its policies.

stroke - a sudden loss of consciousness, sensation, and voluntary motion. This attack of paralysis is caused by a rupture to a blood vessel of the brain, often caused by a blood clot.

veto - the right of one member of a decision-making group to stop an action by the group. In the U.S. government, the president can veto bills passed by Congress. But Congress can override the president's veto if two-thirds of its members vote to do so.

WEB SITES

To learn more about Andrew Johnson, visit ABDO Publishing Company on the World Wide Web at **www.abdopublishing.com**. Web sites about Andrew Johnson are featured on our Book Links page. These links are routinely monitored and updated to provide the most current information available.

INDEX